Storm

# Storm

## Poems by Deb Grant

God's Peace,

*[signature]*

iii

To Stacy

*mi hermana de saliva de ballena*

# TABLE OF CONTENTS

# INTRODUCTION

After moving to the Texas Gulf Coast area for work, I heard the locals tell the histories of their lives. The common threads were names of storms. They spoke like war veterans telling the battles in which they experienced. Within a year of my arrival, I had my own named storm, Hurricane Ike, to mark my story. There were a few more smaller ones until Harvey hit in 2017. Hurricane Harvey was a brute. It wasn't just a coastal event impacting homes and businesses on the shore. Harvey rained on cities of rich and poor, prepared and unprepared. It ripped up small towns on landfall and then it parked for days over Houston dumping 50 inches of rain causing wide-spread flooding. It damaged hundreds of thousands of homes and businesses. It totaled over a million cars. The storms are particularly horrific for the poor, the uninsured, the elderly and the undocumented. The church and the community where I served as pastor was inundated with over four feet of flood water.

What I learned in the years following Harvey is that all storms we encounter in our lives have names. They maybe names that only we recognize, but they are storms, nonetheless. I also learned that our stormed lives are laced with stories of deep pain, surprising joy and relentless love.

I wrote this collection of poems about the hurricane I experienced intimately in the lives of a suffering community. It is my hope that for those who have survived hurricanes this book will be a catalyst for helpful memories of your own resilience. For those who have never experience this kind of disaster, my hope is that these poems will evoke a deeper understanding of what happens to storm survivors beyond the short blink of media coverage. And finally, I hope that these words will be a word of hope and grace for all of us who find ourselves, as Jan Richardson's blessing says, "still within the storm."

Deb Grant

## Blessing in the Storm

*by Jan Richardson*

*I cannot claim*
*to still the storm*
*that has seized you,*
*cannot calm*
*the waves that wash*
*through your soul,*
*that break against*
*your fierce and*
*aching heart.*

*But I will wade*
*into these waters,*
*will stand with you*
*in this storm,*
*will say peace to you*
*in the waves,*
*peace to you*
*in the winds,*
*peace to you*
*in every moment*
*that finds you still*
*within the storm.*

# PROVISION

## ISAAC'S STORM

If you are moving there,
You should read this
As she handed me the book
Which I took because
Who would ever refuse a book?

Learn the lay of the land
The lay
As if living on the Gulf was about land
but a coupling of sea and sand.
Anyone who knows the coast
is like a lover who can tell
one dune-rise from another.
Not even a body of water but more
Like a warm body of gentle skin
Floating above the sheets
While she lifts sun-washed long hair
To the side so that it would frame her
Face on the pillow and silently
Extend the invitation.
There is a lot to love.

The lay of the land.
On this stretch of naked coast,
There have been historical assaults

Not alleged but confirmed.
Storms parting the
Legs of the beach and ripping it in two,
Lifting timbers and battering
Arms raised in defense.
Sea waves foaming at the mouth
Dug their claws deeper into the dunes
Into piers and pillars, porches and promenades
And crushing flesh or pinning it hopelessly
To drown.

If you are going to live on this sacred sand,
It is best to know what happened here.
In 1900.  Look it up.
What happens here.
The horror of little warning.
The foolishness of arrogance.
The heroic failures.
The dunes of debris of whole buildings
Splintered and impaled with death.
To pull off one's shoes and walk the beach
Is to trust a shell is a shell, a stone a stone.
The bodies aren't buried here.
Too many.
They had to burn the ones
They couldn't load on barges.

There is a sacredness about the sand,
The churning, muddy water of the Gulf.
Yes, there are diamond lights dancing as
Engaging diamonds still do
in the angle of the sun,
In the romance of the sea and sand.
To live near it or even to cast one's eyes upon it,
This lay of land,
Is to see both beauty and memorial
To live on and near
this sea-licked land is
to live in a space between
A rape and making love
And to know the difference.

## EVACUATE OR NOT

Decide Decide
Run from the water
Hide from the wind
Storm surge
Flood plain
Last time
First time
Where to go?
What to bring?
How to leave it all behind?
What about the dog?
We can't. Maybe we have to.
Are we monsters if we do?
Decide.
Favorite blanket
Favorite toy
Choose, choose, choose
What to put up high?
How high is safe?
Voluntary Evacuation: we have time
Mandatory Evacuation: make up your mind
Leave now or take this pen to your arm
tattoo yourself for next of kin
One piece of luggage
One trash bag of stuff.

Choose, choose, choose
Who will take us in and for how long?
Decide
Run or hide
Decide
Think think why is this so hard?
Decide.
Run or hide.

## CHECKLIST

The point is survival.
It won't be comfortable
or pretty.
It will last longer than expected.
It will last longer than
patience.

The point is survival.
Potable water
Don't trust the faucet
Expect to get nailed
scraped or broken
or infected or
blown off your feet or
swallow a mouthful of
bayou swill.
Where is the First Aid Kit anyway?
Food – that doesn't need cold to be preserved
or heat to be edible.

And then comes the rest of the checklist
if you have the time and the sense
of knowing a luxury from a necessity
after water, safety, food.
The point is survival.
Not comfort.

The point is survival.

7

## SOLAR FLARE

When the sun burps its gastric indigestion,
it doesn't say excuse me.
It doesn't turn its massive head away.
The flaming viscous phlegm arches from
The surface sending Incendiary splatter
miles into black space.
Most of the time, the flare is not big enough
or targeted enough to reach the face of earth.
What we know is a reduction of its sauce.
Reduced to a dragon's breath of chemicals
That waft unnoticed except by
clever instruments
Or a flicker of electric lights.

Be warned.
The scientists deliver the doom
with a sense of surrender.
One well-directed solar flare
burping in the direction of earth
Will impale the planet with fangs of poison
That will smelt our electrical grid
For years.
Not a temporary outage.
For years.

Disasters happen.
In fire, wind, flood and earth, they come.
The solar flare burps out a possibility
That shakes us out of our disaster doldrums
So accustomed we are to hearing
a hurricane or fire explode in the
News and quickly disappear.
It cannot happen here.

The solar flare tosses a dinner conversation
hypothetical.
How to prepare
For a disaster that has never happened to us.
The first thing, the sudden
Massive, wide-scale power outage.
What would you do?
What would you do first?
What would you do next?
And what after that?
What would you do if the power did not return for
a day or a month?
What news source, if any, would you trust?
What if there was only word of mouth?
How would you feed your family?
Can you trust your neighbor or
the one who says they are?

One solar flare sent in earth's direction.
We would find ourselves
 inside a Twilight Zone episode
hoping for the ending credits to roll soon.
Please tell us it was all just a game.
It could not happen here.
"I can't believe it happened here."
"I can't believe this happened to me."
Disasters fall randomly.
Sometimes there is a warning.
It is never soon or long enough.
How do you prepare for a solar flare?
Or a wind-whipped forest fire,
Or ground shaking cracks into concrete,
Or rivers ignoring their banks?
Sometimes the best we can do is
Ask ourselves what would we do?
Who would we need to help and to help us?
What would we need to survive together?
And make a list. ◧◨

## WATCHING WEATHER

We greet each other
with meteorology.
Feels like rain.
Sure is hot.
Nice weather we're having.

We change the channel.
We surf through a forecast
For clothes decision
Or a trip to the beach or
Work in the yard.

And then it begins,
our masters-level vocabulary
of weather fear.
A piece of cumulonimbus lint
above an African plain.
A disturbance.
A depression.
Moving westward
or tilting north by northwest
or not.
Convection.
Circulation
Pressure.

How long before it finds a coast?
Where will it make landfall?
How big? How fast?

We watch the weather.
We watch the data crunchers
Draw lines
Cones of Uncertainty
We watch it incubate
into a saw blade.
Gale force winds at the edges
Rotating.
An eye filled with a stadium of calm
and winds looking for a fight.

We watch the weather.
We eat spaghetti maps
by the hour.
One jog to the east
the eye will blink away
One jog to the west
We are the monster's target
Pack the family photos
Hide from wind,
Run from water.

We watch the weather
packing, hiding, running
Categorizing our fear.
Cat 1 we need the rain
Cat 2 put the patio furniture in the garage
Cat 3 Stay or Go. Where is the eye?
Cat 4 Go…where? How long?
Cat 5 No, no, no.
We watch the weather.
Through our own turbulence. ▣ ▣

## HOW TO PRAY A HURRICANE

Assume someone listening.
Because at least you are.
And it would be good to find
something useful to say
under our breath
to whoever is listening.

Maybe your prayer can change
its trajectory.
Maybe someone is praying it
away from their house toward
yours. Nothing personal.
Of all the preparation
the shuttered windows
the shopping for provisions
the checking the checklists,
there is no time or energy
for theocracy.

Is there a God who has any power over this?
Is there a God with no power over this?
What's better?
A powerless God
or a ruthless one?
Even our godless prayers to no one in particular

Still look like hope staring at a weather map.
What are we hoping?
That someone else will not be hoping
as hard as we are?

How do we pray a hurricane
Away from ourselves
without losing our compassion
for where it goes?
Do we pray that the storm
will not grow an eye
with teeth hungry for
everything we own?
Do we pray for dominion over
it like a parent to
a temper tantrum?
Sit down, Wind. Shut up.
Go to bed without your supper
Amen. ▪▪

## HUNKER DOWN

An uneasy peace
Is the space when
There is nothing left to do
But shelter in place
Hunker down.

Escape windows are boarded and shut
You were warned
911 listens during a storm but
Does not dispatch.
Don't forget the axe
in the attic
To hack a hole in the roof.

Hunker down
Don't wander outside.
Stay away from windows.
Wait for the power to fail,
the silence of the motors we have to serve us.
How long can the refrigerator
keep the milk and meat
Before we have a somber celebration
Of melting ice cream?

Hunker down and try not
to listen to the wind. ◪ ◪

16

## PORT IN A STORM

When the sky
sullies gunpowder gray
and gust,
where do the birds go?

I want to believe they ride
on a headwind
and find themselves
relocated in another state.

I want to believe that
the birds I see after the storm
blew in on the tailwind
from another country perhaps.
I want to believe they are
bilingual and interesting.

I don't want to think of them
cowering or driven to the ground
or drowning
or broken.
I don't want to think of them
slowly starving.

I want to believe that there are

hummingbirds somewhere
with a Texas drawl
and the ones at my feeder
have Cuban mothers.
It gives me something
to laugh about
during and
after the storm. ◻◻

## EYE OF A HURRICANE

I have stood
in the eye of a hurricane.

It sounds so
earnest.
Hemingway.
Grabbing life by the
Pamplona bullhorns.
Shaking my fists at
the great fish from
the prow
of my little boat.

I did not stand in the eye
to punch a bucket list
or grab bragging rights
or satiate curiosity.

My dog needed to pee.
She approached the
threshold of the door
felt the air with her nose
and froze
and chose instead
to pee on the kitchen floor.

She knew a monster when
she smelled it.

The eye is not peaceful.
The eye is the storm
reloading
and cocking a fist
to punch in the other
direction.

I stood inside the eye of a hurricane.
Then I closed the door.
Cleaned up the pee on the floor
and waited for the
rewind of wind.
Looking for a towel
to throw in the ring
to stop the pummeling
as if I could. ◨◧

# DEMOLITION

## HOME INVASION

Rain comes a monstering
Scraping the panes and siding
Not content to fall perpendicular
Slapping and shattering
nerves already feeling
like a full body root canal

When will the rain stop?
Stop
Another tornado siren
Stop
Drainage ditches choked with debris
Stop

Pavement turns to river
Lawns turn to lakes
Creeping toward the foundation
Seeping under walls and floors
while people watch the water lick
toward the door
from liquid windows by day
by night streetlights over floating cars
flashing headlights and alarms before they
short out and drown.

Too late for sandbags at the door
Too late to stop the water.
Water will find a way.
It is skilled at breaking in
the openings only ants and spiders know.

What to lift off the floor?
What to stack on a counter or a bed?
Surrendering of carpet
Slippering of tile.
Inching up the body to ankle, calf and thigh.

Can food and water be reached sitting
on the kitchen counter?
Could you spend the night there?
Is it time to go to the attic?
Could we climb a ladder and sit on the roof
or climb a tree and wait for rescue?

The rain that slapped at windows
Now an invasion
an enemy relieving itself in your living room with
putrid unmoving lack of care.

A boy in ball cap drives through house
on a jet ski.
Your ride is here.

It's time to go.
Come on, Momma, it's time to go.
It's still raining. ◻◻

## IMPASSABLE

The streets
are veins and arteries
Silent infrastructure
of coming and going
bits of life until they are
rendered impassable.
Obstructed by
a crash,
downed power lines,
or trees.
Flood has no regard for
polite boundaries of
lane lines.
It creates aneurysms then
ruptures.
It is the hypertension
of disaster disease.
Silent. Deadly.
Covering up the dangers beneath
the depth
the ditches
the currents
the sewage
the displaced snakes
or alligators

25

or fire ants.

After the storm passes
there is a desire
to run
to set sail on the arteries
to the heart of other shelter.
To drive the car into the water.
"It can't be that deep."

Passages bleeding out
do not warn
"I am impassable."
It only taunts
"How dangerous do I look
compared to what you are
running from?" ▢▢

## FIRST LOOK

It took two days
for the bayou to recede
within its banks.
Then I could return
to view my present work
my job description soaked
with new duty.

I entered the flooded building
but first it entered me
With the musty mold in
particles small enough to
find their way into my memory.

While distracted by the smell,
my feet found
unfamiliar
slime on familiar floors.

I steadied my step
on the new horizon of
the flood line
Four feet I would guess.

I unlocked my office door
that was swollen shut.
It seemed to push back

like a relative saying
you don't want to see this now.

But I insisted.
I threw my shoulder into it.
Again and again.

At first look, I saw the folly
of my expectation of a flood.
I thought the gentle water
would leak into the building
Rise, soak, lift the plastic
like a person browsing a
yard sale, and then leave
things all in place and wet.

I was wrong.

Particle board bookshelves
melt
sloughing off their laminate and
their load of pages of old friends.
Paper turns to sponge
then dies in one's arms.
Laptops drown silently.
The hardwoods are not spared.
Lovely oak and mahogany
float, soak, shift, lift and
vomit as they fall unjointed.

A flood is a vandal and
a cruel thief.
Not like a fire that burns and ashes.
Not like a tornado that shreds and
sends belongings to the next county.

A flood is the sociopaths
of disasters.

It throws everything worthlessly
at the owners' feet
leaving the precious mess
to be pronounced dead by its loved ones
and carried out to rot in public
and wait for burial. ◻◻

## MEASUREMENTS

The longer the flood water
lingers and
soaks the walls
the more it destroys.
It recedes
and leaves
A room-sized bathtub ring
where the brown swill
reached out with
cruel graffiti
destroying half a wedding picture
or a child's drawing of a bird
or a television
or a door
or a framed degree.

Point the camera at
the water line
with a measuring tape
for proof
for insurance paperwork.

Sear the measurement
into the memory
Whatever the number

by inches or feet
will be tattooed on
the tongue,
ready for the conversations.
The number becomes
the measurement of
our misery and
a number for
our pain and
a way to calibrate
another's pain,
by their number.

Then flood line becomes
the starting place to measure
4 inches above
to make another line
the cut line.
Everything below the cut line
to be sledged and crowbarred
to the studs.

Sometimes there is no cut line
only complete mastectomy
Cut the house to the rib bone
from ceiling to floor
Until all that remains is

emaciation
and measurements. ◫◫

## MUCK & GUT

<u>MUCK</u> [muck] pronounced same as word similar sounding word more UCK.

Derived from Middle English muc, muk <cow dung>

*Noun*

1. Everything you own touched by flood water (not to be confused with water from your tap or your pool. Think river water that has been marinating in sewage, gelatinous chemicals, used diapers and flat beer). Slime is too kind. Muck is more onomatopoeia accurate. All items, paper, plastic, metal, mattress, carpet, wood, the content of drawers and the drawers themselves…become one. Muck.
2. Used in a sentence: Now that everything you own is muck, it must be removed from your house because it is useless at best and deadly at most.

*Verb*

    a. To muck out is to bag, shovel, drag, wheelbarrow everything you own touched by flood water outside in a pile where it becomes a new noun: Debris.

b. To muck out is to have trouble breathing without a mask and to have even more trouble breathing with a mask. It is latex gloves or you will itch for days on end.

c. To muck out is resisting the temptation to look at what you are declaring unsalvageable. You might catch a glimpse of a photo or a child's drawing or a Mother's Day card or your grandfather's pipe now a portrait of black mold destroyed, poison and a memory. To muck out is not to focus much beyond getting whatever you grab into the stretched open mouth of the trash bag.

d. To muck out is to cut soaked carpet with a box cutter into pieces big enough to be efficient, but not so big that a grandparent can't drag outside and not return for more.

e. To muck out a refrigerator is well….nasty. Too nasty for the debris pile. Burn it if you can. Burn it if you can't. The Fire Department will be too busy to hand out citations for code violations.

*[See GUT]*

## GUT

1. As in to be kicked in the gut.
2. As is stripping your house down to its underwear and then that too.
3. Ripping out the soaked sheet rock that clings stubbornly by its nails to studs. Hammers, crowbars, and even being really pissed off helps the work go faster. Insulation is just a sponge for muck – it will endanger the studs that need to dry...that need to breath...that need to be sprayed for mold. Until your living room looks like a bully had come and pulled down the pants of it, exposing the studs and wires. It will look like that for weeks and months. For some, years. Every day the gut punch happens again.

[See DEBRIS]

## DEBRIS

1. Formerly known as everything you own.
2. New name for all the regurgitated flood water ruined contents which were mucked and gutted from your house.

3. Debris piles sit on the edge of the front yard or in the street. Visual and daily reminders that something seriously awful happened here. The piles expand beyond property lines and line the streets to form a canyon of ruined furniture, mattresses, favorite chairs, stuffed toys, water encrusted electronics, shredded carpet and crumbled walls. Shovels are used to carve pathways to the front door or the driveway [See CARS]

4. The source of a smell that grows quickly and lingers. The source of a smell that assaults the sinuses and breaths on your face and down your throat like an itchy sweated wool ski mask a thousand times too small.

5. What you see and smell every day until the city comes with giant claws and dump trucks.

6. What tries your patience and frays your temper because the city is overwhelmed and the piles remain for weeks, months.

## CARS

1. Costly, useful means of transportation

*Variation: Flooded vehicle*

To the wheel wells
might be saved
To the dashboard electronic
Engine

Totaled
Towed
Parked in the infield of a racetrack
or abandoned shopping mall
This hurricane ate
a million cars they say.
Stole mobility
Unless you could afford a rental
Wait on the insurance claim
Buy a new one or
a used one
And hope it wasn't
refurbished
and shipped in
from another flood
out of the country or
out of state. ◻️◻️

## TAKING IN

When the rain stops
the taking in begins
throwing open
the body's windows,
taking in the breath
after holding it for days.
Our senses label and file
and memorize.
>A hood of someone's car
>leans against the toppled tree in the backyard.
>Grind of generators and chainsaws.
>Grills frying meat rescued
>from powerless freezers
>Humid air that feels like a mugger's
>sweat gloved hand
>keeping the mouth shut for fear of not
>knowing how to cry for help.
>A pulled pork sandwich
>and foam-container dish of beans,
>a bag of sour cream and onion chips delivered
>by human hands
>through a food truck window.

Taking in
the fresh truth
of our humanity
intact.

All senses working.
We survived.
We are alive.◻◻

## A DIFFERENT KIND OF DYING

His old frame
of wrinkled cotton
and rolled pants
sweat
on a metal folding chair
in the backyard.

The yard was a canyon
of boxes, tubs,
stacks of household
pieces that had been floating
through the flooded rooms.

This was the sorting time.
The front yard was for debris.
The back yard for drying in the
humid post-storm air.
Queued up for the bottleneck
of decision making.

Each piece
awaits its fate.
Listens for
a diagnosis.
Keep or throw.

Save or pitch.

His hunched attention
on the rusted box
at his feet.
A wrench that was
rusted beyond usefulness
before the flood.
It couldn't hold a bolt then or now
Yet in the folds of his knuckles
vibrates with
its story
like striking a tuning fork,
pleading for pardon.
He can hear his father's hand
from under the truck
"Son, hand me that wrench."
The wrench just needs
a little TLC he says
Puts it in the keep pile.

The box itself however,
is a victim.
Hinges that can no longer hold on
Have chosen to let go.
He carries it like a small casket to
the front yard

lays it to rest.
With a funeral shuffle,
moves his damp sorrow
back to bend over
another backyard box
and drags it without lifting it
to his chair
where he can rest
and start more sorting
before
it rains again. ◻◻

## LOOTERS AND OTHER HUMANS

The human swarm
driving slowly
driver-side windows down
their glance moving from
debris pile
to survivors dragging
broken dreams,
moldy sheetrock
and proud but dead
appliances to the curb

The car moves
more quickly past
the spray-painted
plywood
"Looters will be shot."

Yes, Damn it.
It is trash.
Declared useless
and yet,
the indignity of strangers
picking through the corpses
of their grief and memories
is too much for some.

43

Can't be angry at the storm
so a looter is magnet for the wrath.

Others let go of the debris
more quickly
A glimpse of familiar human need
of common misery.
Why begrudge the discarded bits
to a couple of guys trying to
make a living from metal scraps
or a resale shop?
Buried beneath the debris
is a heartbeat of compassion.
Not enough to paint a sign to say
Looters will be loved
Just enough to catch
the driver's eye
and nod
it's okay
really
it's okay
and look away. ▫▫

## MEAN WELL

The flat screens of chyroned news
Show people shivering
With clothes slathered to their skin.
Eyes fixed beyond their ability to see
What is in front of them.
The shelters taking in
the stormed refugees.

It prompts compassioned
well-meaning aid.
The outpouring of "How can we help?"
There must be something we can do.

Money and volunteers, they hear
But some like to be different
more creative
more personal or thoughtful
I don't know.  I want to think
well of them.
They mean well.
Those who move quickly past
how best to help to
we think we know what's best.
This will make us feel good that
We did something.

A heart of compassion
however it beats even
without thinking
is never to be stifled
Or trifled with.
Never to be judged, refused
Or criticized.
Compassion is encouraged
Is always welcome.
By the truckloads,
at the trigger of the news,
the loads come needing gymnasiums
of space where cots hold
sleepless survivors.

Garbage bags of clothes
gleaned out of closets.
T-shirts faded with logos
of who knows what.
But they are still good,
clean at least most of them.
They mean well.
They mean well.  They do.

Mountains of clothes to be sorted
and offered up.
The clothes demand attention.

Sort, stack, pitch.
Running of out room for both the
people and the clothes.
Move again the stacks and bags.
The calls keep coming.
Where can we send our bags of clothes?
Our box of socks?
They mean well.
We promise to find out, to make some calls.
Who is taking clothes right now?
They were but got too much.
Where the truckloads are going to?

Our box of socks. Our school children gathered
them themselves. They did this all for you. Are you
not grateful? We are teaching our children
compassion. You must help us as we teach them.
You must accept our box of socks.
And we do. They mean well.
We take delivery on the box of socks.
We put it in a corner
until we figure out what to do.
Who needs a box of socks right now?
We move the box from one corner to another
because we need that corner for
Something else.

A pallet of gummy bears.
Really? A forklift full of candy.
For the children, of course.
In this time of stress, they are thinking of
the children.
Where do you want to unload them?
What can we say?
Thank you so much for your thoughtfulness.
For your generosity.
There. In that corner, put them there.
We will figure out what to do with them.

And the box of socks and gummy bears.
While we are still floating in the fog
Of shock and grief and not a little bit of fear.

What can we do to help?
We will not stop their charity.
They mean well.

On a stack of donated shirts
a note was pinned pierced
through our fog of figuring out.
A child's scrawl in colored marker,
"I heard on the tv you lost
all your clothes in the storm.
This is my favorite shirt.

I wanted you to have it.
I hope you like it.
I hope you get better."

They all mean well.
Some even put some thought to it.

## BY DESIGN

Walk a neighborhood at dusk
After dinner or before
What can be seen is by design
A sidewalk, driveway or front door.

A covered porch is rarely seen
By those who pass on evening stroll
Aloneness in a crowded place
Is the master planner's goal.

The porch turned back yard patio
Cedar silo view of just the sky
It could be weeks or maybe months
The random catch of neighbor's eye.

A few defy their architect
And lip the garage with folding chairs
And sit and watch the children play
Patio in place and wave their beers.

Most will honor planner's specs
Castle moat garage doors bridge
To protect our precious privacy
Inside the fence beyond the hedge.

We love our isolated glow
Of lighted screens beyond the shades
We keep our boundaries intact
That is until the storm invades.

Through fire and flood, we fight alike
For house and family just the same
But by design we all are weak
For we don't know our neighbor's name.

## GENERATORS

Noise. Mechanical.
Measured in decibels
Tensing the muscles from neck to jaw.
We pretend it has a beat
But it is just noise.

The engine firing.
Pistons pounding
Gravelly thrumming thrumming
Not a buzz we can swat away

The generators stay outside
To keep the noxious gas outside
To keep the noxious noise outside
like drunken party guests who
stay too long.

So it is defused outside
except the sound
Slams into groans of other generators
Hanging low to the ground
Vibrates through windows.
Into the houses
Where box fans whirl
and slap the air to keep it moving

More noise tolerated.

The sound of survival is
the noise of generators
Generating, vibrating,
irritating as the early morning lawn mowing
Only it never stops.

At night it shakes your teeth
And the back of your brain
where you would rather feel
the silence of your pillow but you can't.

The generator stops when it runs out of gas.
The silence hits us like thunder.
The fan stops fanning.
The refrigerator stops cooling.
The cell phone drains.
Camping inside your own home.
A refill arrives.
The generator fires up again.
Thrumming. Thrumming.
The fan flaps back to life.

The gift of a brief silence is handed back.
Silence can wait another day.
We need the noise of knowing

the air will keep on moving so
we might get some sleep tonight.

Nearby a mother lies
in a ruin without power,
Sleepless, listening to the sound
of generators from neighbors
who do not know her nearbyness
or her name.
She counts hope like pennies
for her children. ◻◻

## TIME TELLING

On pillow, between sheets
Before beats quicken
Eyes turning shoulder shut
To linger in the soft cluelessness of sleep
Time paws the mattress waiting
Like a dog needing to pee.

What day is it?
An easy question
before the storm.
All the days had names and
a playlist of familiar tunes.
Monday slow start and quickened pace.
Wednesday's turn toward weekend.

But this sometime after the storm
Tuesday? Maybe.
Really don't know.
Time with all its measurements
Has dissolved.
Now every day after the flood
starts like a bad dancer
out of rhythm with the music and
the choreography.
Start again…2,3,4 and step 2,3,4.

No, NO!
Start again.

Now time is a binary
Measurement.
Before the Storm
and After.
Before Landfall
and After.
Eyes stay shut longer now.
A little longer
in the twilight time of not knowing
what day it is
a blissful ignorance until
the blare of awareness
it is After the Storm
and not Before. ▨▧

## DISASTER DEFINED

A disaster is when
all you can do
in the midst of it is
measure it
map it
rank it
Count the dead
one at a time or
Hundreds or Thousands
Hope there are survivors
Clean up after it
For years. ◻◻

## TRUTH TIMED

Truth is truth.
Kindness or cruelty is in the timing.

Best and worst advice.
Both rooted in the truth.
But the truth doesn't make it better
Only worth hearing.
Delivering the truth
without decapitating
is about timing.

Recovery will take years.
That is the truth.

Delivered when the last bands of
rain are falling through the roof
onto the family photos
a chair cushion dented with memories
Is nothing short of cruel.

When the dust of drywall mud,
fills the lungs with 'when will it end,'
the truth of stepping outside to
breathe in a blemishless blue sky
divinely timed
life-giving truth. ☐☐

## DISASTER EKG

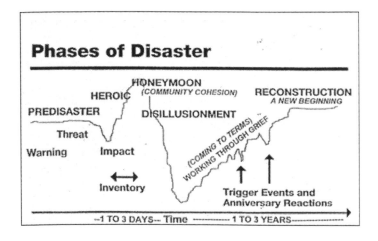

Looks like a heart attack
or a seismograph recording
or a lie-detector test.

Jagged peaks and valleys
ups and downs
For a human heart,
A pattern is good.
A change in the pattern
not so good.
The technician marks
anomalies.
Here is the warning murmur.
Here is the attack.
Here is the response.

Here is the denial,
the aftershock,
or the next attack,
or the setback.
Here is the new pattern
that doesn't look like the
old pattern.
Just different.

The disaster EKG is
Labeled, warning
threat, impact
heroic, community cohesion
disillusionment, coming to terms
working through grief
trigger events, reconstruction
new normal.

It comes into my possession
On an 8 1/2 by 11 sheet, 20lb bond,
copier paper.
It doesn't matter
who puts the paper in my hands
or when.
It gives no comfort
and a little all at once
because this has happened before

and someone survived to tell the
story and graph a beating heart.
I say thank you
Because I don't know
what else to say,
though I am looking at
the EKG wondering
will this patient live?
Will I survive to see
life beyond the EKG? ◫◫

## Nod to God in the Temple of Another

We don't go to church
as much
if we ever did.
Research data points
to reasons without solutions
to fill the pews with nickels
and noses.

We tend to prefer surgery over
change of living.
Cut out the bad.
Label the cancer and
separate it from ourselves.
But that is what the problem
was all along.
We are both
on the cellular level
and are very good
at pretending.

We tend the emptying temples
to a God that we believe
lives there but
who may only stay the
night or two.

Has never called
its stained glass home.

We worship the week
in the temple of another god.
The God of Normal.

We keep our membership
a secret until the wind blows
until the ground shakes
until the wildfires incinerates
until the flood drowns our lives
to a halt and then we
draw our debit card from
our back pockets
to pray
I want my normal life back.

We worship a god who lies to us.
We eat the lies.
Like cane sugar
We feed our cancer
while beyond our infected temples
a scarred yet living hand
of hobo God
dips into an underground river
and holds a cup of water fresh

to a beloved vagabond's parched
and puckered lips. ◻◻

## DEATH TOLL

We can't wrap our heads
around disaster
We can wrap our heads
around numbers
So we count.
The silent tolling
of the numbers
the coroner's report.

What's the criteria for
a storm-related death?
Who makes that decision?
What difference does it make?
How long after the storm
to stop counting?

One Hurricane named Harvey
Death toll: 107
Does not include
broken heart, crushed dreams, utter despair,
delayed surgeries, idiopathic infections.

Deaths reported
Not all bodies found
Swept away

Flash flood
drove into high water
checking on a relative.

Bodies found
in a workplace
floating near a vehicle
floating in a vehicle
floating in a home
floating in floodwater
floating in the ship channel
face down in a parking lot
in a grassy area near a freeway
in a ditch.
Stepped on a wet live wire.
Family of 6 drowns inside white van
(the color of the vehicle was reported)
Drown in his vehicle after ignoring a barricade
the report sounding a warning to the living.
We told you so.
Killed when a tree fell on her home as she slept.
Killed by flesh-eating bacteria after falling and
gashing her leg inside her flooded living room.
Died during a fire in his home during the storm.
Died trying to help
someone who was drowning.
Died because they could not

get to a hospital in time.
Died carrying her 3-year-old to safety. Child was
found alive clinging to her mother's body.

They died inside a death toll
of a named storm that turned
their names into numbers
Except to those who knew
more than their names.
Alexander Batool Travis Agnes Steve Charles Benito
Calvin Andrew Jorge Yahir Colby Benjamin Victor
Ruben Belia Manuel Xavier Daisy Devorah Dominic
Wilma Ruben Martin Michael Keisha Gustavo
Efrain Tomas Samuel Michael Alonso Joseph Jill
Cathy Gary Nancy Ronald Casey Noah Arthur
Donald Rochelle James Bobby Patrick Peter Bonnie
Mary Clevelon Scott Lisa James Joshua Remington
Russell Ginger Collette Roy Dot Richard Clementine
Gene Lee Clifford Michael Sheila Una Timothy
Jimail Francis Ziya Jimmy George Lachlan Ola Mae
2 unidentified infants
No one said they were missing a baby

The death toll includes our humanity
lost and found
in feeling the amputation
and the phantom pain of love

for those who are no more.
As the tolling fades,
we force ourselves to feel the loss
through our self-inflicted anesthetic of numbers to
learn a stranger's name
and story
and how to love again. ◻◻

## STORM OF FORMS

Go with the flow chart
If insured
If not
If owner
If renter
Stand in line
Wait on hold
What's your name?
Address
Policy number
More blanks to fill in
More pages
That file was lost
in the flood
I don't have it
Start again
The fog that sits on
flooded brains have trouble
holding a pen over a page
or keying an unfamiliar
keyboard.
Save Send was it received?
will anyone read it today
or tomorrow?
The wait begins

To fill out more forms
and start again.
Fill out this form
What is your name?
I wish I was just born with
a bar code tattoo
So I could be scanned like
a can of tomato soup
and taken by conveyer belt
to be bagged and carted away
without having to punch my name
into a form where it is so
easily
deleted.

# PTSD

## Part 1: Post Traumatic Stress Syndrome
I stand guard respectfully
by the diagnosis name.
How can a person speak it without humility?
In light of those who first surfaced the disease.
Born inside the firing
human synapses of warriors.
Landmines buried in the ruble of
Human beings disconnected from their souls,
broken down and rebuilt and booted into
Weapons of war.
No longer drafted now
but by their own choosing.
Shipped out, deployed, tours of duty.
What they witnessed,
sealed inside a code inside a cortex.
And then sent home.
Check your weapon at the gate.
At least the one beneath your trigger finger.

Sent back to reclaim their stateside humanity
Baggage claim has it or
You can find it in an airport locker
Where you left it for safe keeping.
Their humanity is never safe.

Ethics are muscles that are
stretched and torn.
Fear is dialed to a red-zone and then
Cooled to sub-human temperatures
in order to pull the trigger,
Launch the missile.
At the target. At the enemy. At the human being.
At the child.
No.
The target. The target. The target.
Gun fire. Explosions. Incoming missiles. Sirens.
Blood.
Triggers for terror,
fight or flight, protect and kill.
Do your duty.
Traumatic Stress happens to warriors
Like none other.
It returns to them as explosive side effect.
Like none other.
Post Traumatic Stress Syndrome
It is an explosive side effect.

Standing graveside,
I have stood where taps played,
A salute gunned, gloved hands folding flags for
Those killed by a private conflict
of self-loathing and fear. PTSD.

The frontlines of unspoken trauma deserve
At least the sole claim on the disorder's name.

**Part 2: Post Traumatic Stress Syndrome –
Disaster**

Trauma is found on other fronts
Where we do not expect to be.
Not war torn
But disaster born
Fire. Flood. Quake. Wind.
Destruction. Loss. Fear. Death.
Trauma comes and leaves behind
Reminders of itself.
Sound of cracking timbers.
Wind.
Smell of mold.
Sting of smoke.
The rain that used to be a sourced of slumber
Now keeps us awake until it stops.

The scars of war are born
no matter the nature of the war.
Disasters create new populations
of post trauma stressed.
No Purple Heart for PTSD.
The civilian has that

in common with the soldier.
There is no medal for
bearing the wound of the soul.
for the sake of serving,
doing the expected job, for surviving.
The landmine planted by the war or storm
lies in wait to be tripped.

I do not speak the diagnosis
Post Traumatic Stress Syndrome lightly.
But respectfully.
In a whisper.
Lest I disturb my own.
Or yours. ▢▢

# RESILIENCE

## FIRE ANTS

Fire ants
Their thirty-five day lives are spent
Surviving.
Their only thriving is done
In the dry heat and sudden rain
Finding food
Framing dirt
And tending to their replacements.
A massive operation.
They are built to move in mass.
They colonize. They teem. They swarm.
Defensive action is to bite.
A single bite is annoying.
A swarm could fell a deer.
Singularity is not even a luxury.
They could not survive alone.

Every rain surfaces their disaster plan.
They are built to survive a flood.
As the flood rises, the ants take action.
Linking ant legs and mouths,
they weave themselves
Into a raft in a minute
moving queen and Infants
to the center in the highness and dryness

Of their now seaworthy community.
A buoyancy of bodies
with fine hairs trapping just enough air
barely breaking surface tension
Keeping the whole colony afloat
Until the ark of their covenant
Arrives, not back home again,
But on new dry land.

Wading humans lifting and pulling legs
Through flood waters
Are warned of floating fire ant mounds.
The rafted colony is fully armed.
Locked and loaded for survival
They are ready to pull the trigger and
Light a fire on the flesh that water
Cannot douse or sooth.

Humans are warned to watch.
Steer clear
Of the drifting rage of rafted ants.
Keep your distance.
Leave them to their disaster plan.
You tend to your own.

Our disaster plan if there is one
Starts as one. One person. One household.

Our plan is to climb away alone
or walk out alone.
We drag our wet legs alone
Through the thigh deep sewage avoiding
The dangers we can see.
Unaware of the dangers
To which we cling.

The fire ants float with the current,
linked by legs and mouths
Accepting their need for
and responsibility
To one another.
It comes naturally to them.
The rest of us drag our wet legs
Into the truth that
we need each other.
Or we navigate alone and
Steer clear of both the
ants and their lesson
of intimate survival. ▣▣

## RESILIENCE DEFINED

Rubber band.
Adaptability.
Give as in slack in rope
or room to breathe.

Yield sign in the States
Is Give Way in New Zealand.
Give way without
Giving up altogether.

A pinball that keeps moving.
Though I don't know
at any given time if
I am the ball, the paddles
or the controller?
All of the above.
Pliability.
Elasticity.
Tenacity.
Endurance.

A mattress of memory foam.
I try to remember who I was
And find that shape again.
The dents of the damage

though remain.

Resilience is to shape the dents
into new memories.
Death-dealing wounds never
grow up to be scars we live with.
Resilience is learning
there is within us
a will to live,
to find a way
to live with
the stretch marks
and the scars. ◻◻

## FLY THROUGH THE CRASH

In the aftermath
When the buzz saw bands
on the radar maps
are less angry red.
When the monster is downgraded to
A depression.

Then comes the wave of well-meaning advice
From friends and strangers
From veterans of other storms
They bring out their storm stories like
A soldier's chest of campaign ribbons.
I am in the cockpit of your own doomed flight,
a trajectory that spirals down.

With knuckles exposed on
The controls, I listen through static headsets
For some words with meaning
Some advice that might be worth
The air that it is traveling on.

Take care of yourself.
Get some sleep.
Don't forget to eat.
Pace yourself.

81

Get your forms in right away.
Keep after them.
Be the squeaky wheel.
You know what I mean.
You gotta be the squeaky wheel.
Or maybe, you're not up to it.

And then I hear it.
The highly oxygenated words
of serendipity
I needed to pluck them
out of the wind as they fly by.
From someone who lived through tempests
And sought to help more than
suck all the air away or
create a pocket of more turbulence.
It wasn't original to her
but they helped her
so she tossed them in the wind
In my direction and I caught it.
"Fly through the crash."
"Fly through the crash," she said again.
"You might just land the plane."
And I did.
Thanks be to God.
I did. ▫▫

## MOSES MANN

"It coulda bin worse."
He says with a shake of his head
Spilling out over bad teeth
A smile and a sigh.
Looking at you right in the eye
So that you know that even if you
Doubt the things he says
That, that is the God's honest truth.
"It coulda bin worse."

Four feet of rain
Turned his house into an island
but wanted more of him
and so turned to soak the ground beneath.
This foundation where he grew up
with mother and siblings.
The first night the house was surrounded
The second night the ground
beneath the house turned to mud
The walls soaked up the sludge.
The walls strained against wood and nails
Creating fissures small
and blood brown on the walls.
Enough to do more damage than
a coat of paint.

Moses can still hear the house groan.
The house where he grew up groaned.
"Never forget that sound" he said.
His eyes disappeared into the
Dark thought until...until....
there it was again...
a light.
A light in his eye
looking smack at you.
His face tickled with it.
The smile and sigh
the shake of his head.
"It coulda been worse."
He said. ◘◘

## THE COURAGE OF THE EARTH

Not all tree trunks
grow up as trees
are meant to do when
they are free to be,
ready to branch
when the mystery of their molecules
decide its roots can bear more
opportunity of leaves.
Supply and demand.
The economics of
A single tree or forest.

But some are grown
around obstacles thrown.
A trunk with scarred bark
belly wrapped around
an old barbed wire fence or
a rope or metal post.
A camera might with patience
capture the time-lapse resolve
of the tree to shape itself around or
absorb the obstacle into itself.

Then there is a tree
thick and round, close to the roots

anchored to the earth's core.
But before it was shoulder high,
something happened.
Something turned or cracked or bent it
horizontally.
It grew sideways until
it decided to walk upright again
and find the sun.
Each increment of growth
weighing the balance of
not being centered over its roots.

What happened to you?
How did this deformity form?
Was it a storm?
Was it an angry boy bent on cruelty?
I cannot speak for you, only for me.

Is this what is happening to me?
Broken but alive.
Finding a way to grow
with a broken bone that set itself
before any surgery could help.

The earth does what it can
to heal its scars and insist on living.
The flowers that pushed months after

volcanic ash smothered the ground.
The tree that knows it is broken
and yet still finds its feet
and limps toward the sun.
What courses through
a broken tree,
courses through me.
The earth feeds us
with hope
when we acquire
a hunger for it. ◻◻

## COPING

We try on coping skills
like eyeglass frames.
Choices that are ours to make
on how to move hour by hour
through these post-disaster days.
The method itself can
change the path,
suck energy,
drown us again in despair,
create resolve and
not a few surprises.

Pollyanna.
It's all good.
Never mind the mold growing up the wall.
Never mind the phone for help on hold.
Isn't the music lovely!
Look for rainbows.
This requires the magic
of perfect timing.
To speak such light out loud may
actually, lift a moment
Or else spark a bitter grenade
"Leave me the hell alone."

Pessimist.
It's all bad.
Life is a struggle,
then we die.
No one will help.
Why should they?
Who cares?

Is there a way to speak truth
without hurting?
How necessary is the truth
right now?
There is always
the empty default answer
"It is what it is."
It speaks a truth.
It does no harm
and no good.

Squeaky wheel
The crisis management approach.
Attend to the one closest to one's line of sight.
Whoever is making the most noise.
Repeat it over and over
again until the one making
the most noise is you.

A return to wholeness is not made by
surgically removing
the bad news from the good.
How to embrace both
like warring siblings.
Sometimes it means lashing
yourself as to a yardarm,
to stay with the ship
to sail it to safe harbor
after the storm or
go down with it
because that is the truth of it.
The soul adjusts to
a balanced diet of
hope and fear.

Sometimes we don't discover
how we survived
until we have.
Until we are out of the wind
repairing our sails
or looking back on
the path we carved
and only then we speak of
what we know or
leave stacked stones on the path
to tell others where to go. ◨◨

## DID YOU KNOW THAT?

- A hymn book that has soaked three day in flood water swells to 3 times its original size.

- Copier sales teams deploy after a storm to visit flooded offices. They come in crisp, clean polo shirts with an embroidered patch and a business card that lands upon their departure on the floor slime.

- People will come by offering prayers. And maybe a sandwich. The sandwich and a bottle of water could taste like bread from heaven, cup of salvation from a disposable chalice. The prayer is nice too.

- "Sheetrock" is a brand name for drywall. That not all wallboard is the same as drywall. That some boards are made of gypsum that is mined from a vein that arches through America and created jobs and planted towns of growing up places. That some drywall is water-resistant, but they will never say waterproof. Thick drywall is good for building. Thin wet drywall is easier to rip from the studs.

- Within a couple weeks your friends who live the next state over will wonder why you aren't finished cleaning up after the storm.

- Trees and plants don't like saltwater. Neither do refrigerators, or stoves or computers.

- Toilets can survive a flood. They deal with shit all the time and clean up well. A working toilet is a gift outright not to be denied at any time to anyone.

- Before throwing the waterlogged hymnal on the debris pile, a guy lifted one up and said, "Hey it's not all bad…. we have more hymns to sing now!" and we laughed. What we didn't know before…. kept us from drowning.

## THE HAIR SALON

The hair salon sat
Uniquely high on Main Street
Across from houses,
other businesses,
other places of worship,
other restaurants.
All crippled by the flood.
All unable to do business.
All fearful of no population
to sustain any business for
months or ever.

The salon sat strangely high
on mound crowned
with its small building,
surrounded with pavement.
The elevation saved it
from the flood.

Dry and powered
and staffed.
Open for business.
But who would come to
have hair done
in the middle of a disaster?

93

We watched from across
the street.
A steady busy-ness of
customers came.
Little white women mostly.
Wisps of white, thin hair
Frail, halting, stepping
out of large sedans.
Some with a caregiver.
Some with a metal walker.
Managing the incline from
the parking lot to the parlor door.
All day.
Every day without a lull.

While debris piles grew
with the despair along the street,
the customers came.
It had to be more than the
shampoo or the do.
More likely, it was the bliss
of keeping an appointment.
It was swivel chair of normal.
One normal hour at a beauty shop.
One normal day above the fray.
Rarified air of beauty product
and denial for a little while.

They bought what could be sold
In a salon above the flood. ◫◫

## INSIDE OUT

The streets are
canyons of debris
that merge from one
yard to the next.
Each house has
vomited what once
had been the comfort
of a recliner or a
mattress, the convenience of
a chest of drawers.

From the outside,
the house looks whole
bricks and window frames
intact.
After the claw truck removes
the household puke,
there is the appearance of
almost a normal neighborhood.

Inside the house
is stripped of insulation
and carpet.
Like a bully had grabbed the walls
by the waist and pulled them
down to their ankles.
Skinny studs embarrassed

96

and no match for wind and
noise blowing through the
siding.

Inside a family camps
in the center of a living room
with unkind concrete
lit by a table lamp sitting on
the floor.
A small child
peers out the flaps of
a pup tent where the
sofa used to be.
Parents making dinner
on a hot plate.

Driving by,
you would not see
how the storm damage is
not yet repaired.
Nor witness the
courage of a family
living
an interrupted life. ◨◨

## TURN, THEN, AND LIVE

"I take no pleasure
in the death of anyone."
A scripted voice is
quoted when we reach
the end our hope
dangling over
our demise.

I heard it
rounding up cattle
with friends.
I had no business
rounding up cattle
it just sounded like
an adventure

The task of the day
was confining cows
between gates
to tag them.
I was in the wrong place
at the wrong time.
Face to angry bull snout.
No one could move
fast enough to help me.

98

Frozen in place.
I heard a voice say
"Turn, then, and live."
Well, not quite with
such biblical eloquence.
The voice said,
"Don't let him hurt you!"
Amygdala, arise!
Victim or Survivor.
Choose.
Now.

I found a vertical leap
I have never been able to repeat
Until I faced a flood
after a hurricane
until I was at the end
of my hope
and
chose to live.
Don't.
Call me.
A victim.

## HELP AND A THIN PLACE

Help.
I need help.
Now is not the time to ask me
why I didn't evacuate
or why I didn't prepare sooner.
I am in my attic,
on my roof,
with my children
and a dog.
I am clinging
to a tree in my front yard
in my car
in a wheelchair
I need help.
Please help.

Help came in helicopters
and aluminum boats
The heroes surfaced
in young ball-capped faces
in flat-bottomed boats.
Left hand on the tiller
and leaning forward.
Holding your wet dog as you
boarded with your luggage of

a garbage bag.

Help came on jet skis
through the front door
of your grandma's house
to extend hand and "Yes, ma'ams"
on to a kind of horse
she's never seen up-close.
Arms wrapped around the
the back of a stranger's grandson
riding off into a sunset
to shelter.

Help came in the side window of
a van with a hand
offering a bottle water,
a sandwich, a prayer.

Help came in the restaurant that
threw out the menus and the bill
to feed the uniformed and all those
ballcapped heroes.

Help came in achurch
that took in a neighbor's flooded flock.
A place for water-logged souls to gather
To see familiar faces with understanding eyes

101

and feed on bread and wine,
to sing their cold hope back to life again.

Help came.
The stories are good to tell
even when the air is heavy
with the sorrow of tomorrow.
The stories of the help and
the heroes are still there and
good to hear again.
The stories help.
They offer a thin place to
stand and press our noses
against the glass and see
again from a place of safety now.
What we saw then
Heaven in motorboat
and the muscle-memory
of our own smile. ◻◻

## DREAMS

"What do you need?"
Beside a house repaired,
the nightmare over,
your life back intact.

"What do you need?"
without kitchen yet, but
enough money for takeout.

"What do you need?"

He said,
"I want to wake up
in the middle of the night,
pad down the stairs
into my kitchen
and make myself
a grilled cheese sandwich."

After a flood,
dreams are undiluted
wants and needs
close enough
to taste
in our sleep. ▣▣

103

## THE LONG AND SHORT

Disasters are a short news cycle.
Suddenly, a headline.
And just as quickly, not.
The reporters packing cameras
and business cards
from ABC
and Reuters
and the New York Times
swarm
and listen over your shoulder
at the next storm, or
fire, earthquake.
Making deadlines
Filing stories by 5 o'clock.
The name of the town will
fall out of mention in a day or two
while the aftershocks last for years.
The storm is not short
or ever over.

Inside a church meeting hall,
around long tables end to end
men and women gather
from agencies of help.
A county commissioner,

a parish priest, a psychologist,
a guy with a boat and time on his hands.
A small town's Situation Room
They come uniformed, suited,
shirts with embroidered logos,
clergy collars and
armed with notebooks.
Armed to help.
Willing to fill forms for big money
and find big muscle.
Ready to shoulder the
Long haul of it.
In between their pre-storm
jobs and homes of their own
to muck and gut or
feel guilty in because
they didn't flood.

Willing to try,
fail and try again.
To get their neighbors
back in a home that is
Safe.
Sanitary.
Functional.

After the meeting adjourns,

they linger.
Huddle over one case,
one family story,
if they can pull together
for just this one and
and then again tomorrow.
That is stride of the marathon
Not the sprint of
Long term recovery.

Life is short.
Love is long.
That is
the long and short of it.

**IMPACT**

Waves of a storm's impact
are relentless
long passed landfall
it leaves heavy-handed
fingerprints.

Trees choking on
saltwater water surge
die slowly.

The birds, the butterflies, the beetles
lose habitats they cannot rebuild.

Earth's wetland kidneys wilt with
the toxic mix of salt and sewage.

The oysters have no gems of food
to turn into a living wage
for a fisherman or a waiter.

A teacher displaced from home travels hours
to keep her job.
Losing time and sanity in transit.

Gentle window rain

107

triggers a temper quicker
than lulls one into sleep.

An infant's brain is washed with
too early lessons of fight or flight.

The local family grocery closes.
A victim of not enough families close-by with
working kitchens.

A storm's impact
is measured in the scars
of a person or a town
or in the hidden will
to rise up against
the daily storms
to push aside the
curtain of despair
and throw seeds
of kindness in the air. ▢▢

## FIRST ANNIVERSARY

*But take care and watch yourselves closely, so as
neither to forget the things that your eyes have seen
nor to let them slip from your mind all the days of
your life. -Deuteronomy 4:9*

The anniversary of a hurricane
Triggers sorrow.
The wound is not yet healed.
The calendar is a cruel
reminder of what we
want to forget,
of what we have yet
still to do.

Fear that broke into
our homes like thieves
and toyed with our
security.

The smell of mold
growing up the walls
and into the air
into our bodies
stealing our breath
and health.

109

The bureaucratic minefield
to get help
only shown more forms.
You can't pass Go.
Return to Start Again.
A board game monopolizing
a person's will.

The suffocating slow torture
of an old woman
living in a damaged house
facing a southern summer
without a fan to move the air.

The anniversary also comes
with storied lights
that defy the ashes
and the mud.
The boatman's hand,
the gift of food
the bottled water
shoulder high.
The face of every single saint
who said
"What can I do right now for you?"

This date I choose again
to see
the eyes of grace
the color of the sky
and the smell of fresh paint.
There are some things
that storms and the flipping
of a calendar
cannot steal.

## SHOW ME AGAIN

Unblemished blue and up
Enough to stretch the neck
spent looking too much down.
The sky clapped my attention
with the shout of color
as I stepped out of the clutter
of my crumpled chores.

Emerging from workers'
construction dust.
Taping, floating, sanding.
Eyes stinging crusty with
the necessary steps of restoring walls
and ceilings to keep out the
sky and the weather.
I saw through damp eyes
a brand new shade of blue.

It is good
to turn oneself inside out
and blink oneself aware
to something, someone
bigger than ourselves
who is doing
amazing things.

While we are preparing
putty walls,
it is good to step out into
the hushed Sistine chapel
of the dome of earth.
The breath and the wonder
of it makes us better.
It pokes a hole through
a dusty soul,
clears our lungs
flexes our muscles
of praise to say
"Show me again,
Creator of that
hue of blue,
Show me again."

## THE HAVES AND THE HAVE-NOTS

The storm
threw us all together
in the swill of our
common crisis.

It didn't last
the togetherness
The sorting out
The lines blurred
by the flood
were drawn again
in the mud.
The lines form on
one side of the line
and the other.

At first the differences
were clear.
Cash in hand.
Insured.
Savings for a rainy day.
Line of Credit.
Wink and a nod
of who you know.
The ones who cut in line

and call it suffering
because they've never
had to wait in line.

The storm marks the poor.
The unconnected.
The vulnerable to
to greedy pockets.
The poverty of documents
that flinches when
a stranger is at the door.
The bleeding memory of
those who can't remember
a number or a name.

It looks the same on the surface
as it did before the storm
the Haves and the Have Nots
and yet
a glimmer of a difference

Among certain pockets of poor
a tender community whispers
"We are in this together."
I have dry wall to spare.
Stay in my home, while you wait.
Eat with us, you and your kids tonight.

115

We poor are imperfect.
We get angry and jealous.
We still have hearts
that beat for our neighbors
and offer what a piece
of who they are.

After the storm,
the wealthy rebuild quickly
and tell stories of how long
they had to wait.
After the storm,
the poor are still poor
and know the worth
of what they have
and who their neighbors are.

After the storm
the Haves and the Have Nots
are still there.
Some have neighbors.
Some have not. ◨ ◧

## REBUILDING VOLUNTEERS

A house on the corner
of the church property
was rental property.
It had flooded like the rest.
The sanctuary its purpose and affection
in the eyes of worshippers.

The house had lost its purpose
Until it held a dream of possibility.
Rebuilt it could be used
to house the volunteers
who would come for years
to the neighbors one by one.

Before the storm it was real estate,
property, a source of income
After the storm it recruited,
Damaged but repurposed
Called to service.

After the storm, it was my job
to turn away from
the demands of worship space
to make the short trek
beyond the parking lot

to the house where disciples came
to rebuild the house offered to
house more disciples called
to serve.
The volunteers moved
from doors
 to debris
to saws and wood
to benches in the shade
to sandwiches
and back to work again.

Introverted by nature I am
but this was not a time
to let nature have its way.
The storm took
more than its share
of my preferences.
I walked across the parking lot
and thrust my hand into
their sweaty, dusty ones
and I thanked them.

They offered bits of their stories.
Where they were from.
The places blurred together on
a map of states.

What they did for a living.
Student, retired something,
veteran, raiser of children,
Driver of buses, farmer of Christmas trees
and a maker of bacon.

I told them how the house they
were rebuilding would be used.
I told them the house was coming
alive with their fingerprints.

Always I asked them
why did they come?
why did they come at their own expense,
drive for hours and nights,
to eat mediocre sandwiches
and sleep on church hall floors
to do work they don't normally do
for people who they have never met
or will likely ever see again.
Why did you come?

Some shrug as if they don't know
for certain themselves.
The thread of an answer
often was the tender cord
of a relationship.

A friend, a lover, a soldier,
a traveler of an extra mile
that had shouldered tears or
weight for them.
A kind of paying forward.
A combination of an invitation
and some time on their hands.
A pleasant memory of a previous trip
with these same travelers.
Because you needed help.
Because you needed help.
It was what God wanted me to do.
It is just what people do.
The right thing
because a need
makes a neighbor,
near or far,
known or unknown.
Because a need
makes a neighbor
hold fast to hope.

Provoke one another
to love and good deeds.
The volunteers
wore encouragement
on their dusty sleeves

and brushed it off on
me during a prayer
huddle of woven arms
and shoulders.

They went back to work.
Thanked.
I walked back to my other work
across the parking lot
dusted with their
tenderness
and laughter.
I tucked the hope
inside my pockets
where I would forget
their names but
not why they came.
I would remember
why they came
as I became
a volunteer.

## THIS MARIA

This Maria
Stepped from the car
with a curly haired boy in hand
and a baby riding her hip.

She was a thousand mothers
who walk in silence
bearing the daily weight
of the beloveds.

This Maria
single mother
7 children beneath her wings
2 lost their parents
to death and deportation.
This Maria
took them in.

This Maria
hunkered down
with her children
in a fragile house
that the storm
lifted from its foundation
and cracked.

Spilled out into currents
with evicted snakes and
gators, this Maria
waded her children to
a dry shelter and
an uncertain future
with an effervescent
hope that rose from
the sides of her despair
like bubbles of champagne
she could not afford
so she became the
wealth of crystal-stemmed hope
for her clan.

This Maria
sought and found
help for her broken home.
Angels came in the form
of retired men with extra time
and big hearts.
Angels came in the form
of young people with strong backs.
Angels came from beyond
stained glass to where Jesus
spends his time

Angels brought a house
on the old foundation.
Angels brought floors and paint,
Dishes and beds.
Angels brought a homemade quilt
an heirloom from another family to
give her house a piece of history amongst
the newness. A comforter of family love.
Angels brought a Bienvenido mat
to lay before the door of a house
made whole after the storm.

Today was move-in day.
18 months after the storm.
Maria and the Angels worked.

This Maria
stepped from her car
like a thousand other mothers
with the weight of children in hand.
But today
This Maria
danced.

This Maria is
still poor today.
All the pre-storm struggle

on her shoulders
All the children still beneath her wings
with all the fears and sorrows
But today she
moves between the air and pavement
as if lifted on unseen wings
teaching her children
how to be grateful
how to act in the presence of angels
teaching her children
how to dance. ▫▫

# EXHORTATION

## DEEP BOW

The storm evicted
one pastor to the
altar on the higher ground
of another priest.
Two holy women
different flavored
one more refined in liturgy
the other less so,
but the storm makes
one a good guest,
the other a good host.

Roped into white robes
and yoked with
the color of the season,
they stood together
facing forward at the front
in a moment of
public reverence
to the presence
of the One whose mystery held
no answers during a storm,
yet still a tether to survival
for fraying faith and
wordless prayers.

The liturgical words
were familiar for both,
but the gestures were a language
the pastor didn't speak so well.
The priest would bow
sometimes with the head
and a slight lean from the waist.
Sometimes, on high holy days,
the bow was deep from the waist
until the crown of the human head
was fully pointed at the divine presence
at the altar.

Storms flood one's pores
with new vocabulary,
raw emotions,
new bitterness,
and sink holes of despair.
And just as certainly, it brings
a thousand new reasons to be grateful
and even a few new ways to show it.
The pastor learned to bow.

The priest bowed because it was
her intimate and holy gesture of gratitude,
a wholly necessary step of choreography

of a dance of music and mystery.
The pastor bowed, at first,
to be a good sport.
It was awkward.
Like a reluctant teenager
being forced to kiss the cheek
of an obnoxious aunt.
The priest hip-checked her
yoked sister
and chuckled.

The pastor learned to bow,
because the reasons for being grateful
recovering from the storm
were more vast than
the words, or the prayers
or the linens on the altar
or the taste of bread
or color of the wine in the
brass chalice,
or the organ music swelling through the air.

Thank you was the first and last thing to say.
But never enough.
Never enough.
Sometimes it was all
that could be done was

dance with palms pressed together
and hearts bent to the holy ground.
The ancient liturgy
is a way of moving
through storms of every form.

The mystery is not solved, but
we can learn a new language,
a new posture,
in its presence,
bowing deeply,
befriended,
grateful,
and alive. ◻ ◻

## HOLDING SPACE

When tears or terror
splash out,
when faces grimace
and eyes flood themselves
into blindness
words sit down
in the presence of pain.

We don't know
what to say to comfort.
We know what others say
that harms, that we ourselves
have said to fill the void of
not knowing what to say.
We want to take our leave
without waking them so
they won't see us leaving
them alone.

There are, however, winged ones
Who seem to know that those wings
are not for flight, but for
holding space.
It is an art of valor
to hold the space

where the inflammation
of human suffering
is still burning.
The wings do not
have answers
or healing balm.
They are feathered walls
for fists to pummel without
offense.
Holding space
creates a new air
where hope can catch its breath
where even the whispered words
"It's okay."
"It's going to be okay."
Uttered with love may be
more truth than lie.
Where courage can be a promise
to be tried on
like a stranger's coat
placed on your shoulders
while sitting in a lifeboat
or a shelter or sitting on the curb
of a life burnt to the ground.

To hold space for another
is to use our wings to

acknowledge that pain and life
cannot be separated,
cannot be solved,
or consoled,
but can be held.
It can be the scarred arms
of you are not alone.
Be the resistance
against the vacuum that
wants to crush you to fill the void.
It can be a safe space to flail around,
to be given freedom and dignity,
to give birth to a new courage,
in one's own time.

Some helpers of the storm
came with wings
they didn't even know
they had and yet they used
to hold the space.
To be a shelter
For a human heart
Rebuilding from the inside out. ◻◻

## A Bird in Hand

A reflection of sky
in a window
confuses birds.
They fly full speed
into a glass wall
with a single knock
that sets the dog to barking.

If the bird has survived
the crash,
it lays off its feet
still and dazed,
Willing perhaps to climb
on anything like a branch or
a finger or held in a hand
and have the infinitesimally small
feathers of its head
stroked tenderly.

The storm is like
a window to a bird.
It confuses us.
Disorients us.
Disrupts us.
Threatens us.

135

After impact,
we are either death count
or stunned survivors willing
to perch for a while
on an extended hand
while we find our feet again.
While we catch our breath
or stop holding it.
While we clear our sight.
While the gale force of our fear
sits down.

We perch
accepting crumbs of food,
a bottle cap of water,
a stroking of our feathers,
until we discover
we are alive.

We can move.
We can feel our feet
and open our wings.
We choose a bit of sky.
We feel the gravity of our fear
and the echo of pain
thrumming through our bones.
We remember we can fly.

## PICKING UP THE PIECES

"What keeps you going?"
The question came from those
outside the storm
to those still inside it.

Joy.

I didn't not have to hesitate or ponder.

Joy.

I imagine
when God created joy for us
it was as big as the firmament sounds
vast like living in a coffin-sized room
and suddenly opening a door into
a stadium bigger than a city
or an ocean-sized infinity pool
on the edge of the star-cloudy universe
With lilies of the valley everywhere
and white pelicans and ladybugs.

For whatever reason,
that dome of joy shattered
into shards.
The kind that
break by design into tiny

harmless pieces without
lethal edges.
Rather like uncut
diamonds sitting on the pavement
or in the grass
or in your pocket
waiting to be found.

Joy after the storm
comes in pieces
that don't hurt but shine
like a firefly.

We discover we
still know how to laugh.

A crayoned card
that says, "I am sorry about the storm
that hurt you. I hope your house gets better."

A young man singing
"A Bridge over Troubled Waters"

The white linen of a restaurant oasis
stemmed crystal holding a California merlot
and a fox-hole friend.

The smell of paint and the thud-bang of
a carpet layer's tools.

Every pair of eyes that sparkled over
masks and work gloves.

Any meal that needed utensils.

A phone call from a frozen land laced with
Minnesota nice and a promise that
help is on the way.

Joy comes in pieces
after the storm,
still bright
and big as God's dream,
but small enough
to hold
to let its energy
push against
the wall of the past
now soaked in grief
and the future looming with fear.

Joy comes in pieces
and creates
a present of the present.
In this new bright
Universe of Now
We feel God's masterpiece.

We are here.
We can find ourselves
on the original blueprints.
We are here.
We can hold the universe
in our hand and
laugh out loud
at the unexpected
delight of being alive
and so graced.

The joy pieces
held in the present,
in our hands,
held out like offerings,
holding the glistening
we cannot imagine without help.

The pieces turn to water clear and
splash into our palm
and through our pores
and course through our veins
and become who we are.
God's resilient children
made of light
and shards of dreams
still yet to be.

To recognize
a piece of crystal joy
within the storm is
how we find
our way
home again.

**STORMS HAPPEN**

Storms are named.
The names are recycled
Except for the bad ones.
Those names are retired.
They have done so much damage,
their names trigger memories
for those who soldiered
that battle and
wear a ribbon inside their chest
for surviving that campaign.

There are other kinds of storms
named in the wrinkle of a memory
by a date
or a place
or a personal earthquake.
The day dad died.
The doctor's office test results.
Love ending.
Name your loss,
Your chaos,
Your storm.

Storms can level us.
They change us from
the inside out.
They change our trajectory.

They bombard us with
grief and fear.

Storms can teach us.
Storms knock us off our feet.
We start again as infants,
discovering our fingers
and our toes
and recognizing the face of love.
Discovering what we can do
with our feet and our hands
and our love.

Storms happen.
Often.
Disaster is the norm.
Surviving is our lives.

Prepare for the next one.
Pack love.
Lots of it.
Enough for yourself,
Family and strangers.

Storms happen.
They come with names
So does love.
Love comes with your face
and your name.

# Acknowledgments

I am grateful…

To Jan Richardson for permission to use her exquisite painting "Still in the Storm" for the cover and her poem "Blessing in the Storm" in the introduction of this book.

To Carol Sonnenburg, friend and encourager who copyread the manuscript for me.

To Heath and Erika Abel and their daughters Alex and Elli who splash my life with unconditional love and are ridiculously supportive of my writing life.

To Nancy Davis for her guidance into my retirement and into this new adventure.

To all the people of the Texas-Louisiana Gulf Coast Synod of the ELCA who participated in the recovery of Faith Lutheran Church, Dickinson, Texas and many other churches and sites in the community after the storm.

To the people of Holy Trinity Episcopal Church and Faith Lutheran Church who served for a season in the same boat using what we had and doing what we could for the sake of other in need.

To the Hurricane Recovery staff of the Episcopal Diocese of Texas: The Rev. Stacy Stringer, Kécia Mallette, and Suzanne Hollifield. They have given me the opportunity to hear and tell the stories as they assist the most vulnerable ones who are still recovering from hurricanes.

To the St. Philip's Disaster Relief team of St. Philip's Lutheran Church, Fridley, MN. They traveled many miles, several trips, to help people. They serve with compassion and joy. SPDR understands that storms happen all the time and the journey continues to answer Christ's call to love our neighbors.

To The Rev. Stacy Stringer for being my Whalespit Sister, a companion for justice, an advocate for the most vulnerable, a companion in capers and a source of relentless joy.

Deb Grant

## How to help after a STORM

1. Disasters come in all shapes and sizes. The death of a loved one or a hurricane.
2. Know that it is not as simple as this sounds, but this is a good place to start.
3. To respond with compassion and wisdom, tennis great, Arthur Ashe once suggested the following:

   - **Start where you are.**
   - **Use what you have.**
   - **Do what you can.**

   This is good advice whether you have been impacted by a disaster or want to help those who have.

4. If you are witnessing those impacted by disaster like a storm, fire, earthquake and want to help:
   a. Send money: pick a trusted source.
   b. Do not send items that are NOT REQUESTED. Storage and sorting of these items become a burden for those you are trying to help.

c. Wait before traveling to a disaster area. While you are waiting, consider learning new skills such as power tool usage, flooring, drywall installation and compassionate listening. When you come, come with a group that has arranged their own housing, food and work sites. Research on the internet guidance to volunteers and help the group prepare what to say or not to say to survivors. Read poems of STORM, to help volunteers feel and discuss what they hear.

d. Look through the eyes of the homeowners', not your own. Your priorities of what is important to rebuild or fix may not be the same as yours.

e. The opportunity to see the repair work finished is a rare event. You can't make it perfect or prevent disasters from happening again.

f. Know that the gratitude may not be expressed or reach the level you might need, but rest assured...your help is deeply needed and much appreciated.

# About the Author

Deb Grant is a human living under the laws of gravity in Houston, Texas. Grant is the author of 5 previous books, Pedestrian Theology, ELOGOS Daily Devotions for Down to Earth Disciples 1,2, & 3, and Passage. This book is her first book of poetry.

A native of New England, Grant earned her undergraduate degree from Barrington College (now Gordon College). She earned a Master of Divinity from Trinity Lutheran Seminary, Columbus, Ohio. Grant was ordained in 1981 serving as a pastor and campus pastor in the Evangelical Lutheran Church in America. After 37 years in ministry, Grant retired. She continues to write, create art pieces, care for her friends and help with hurricane recovery. Joy arrives daily for Deb in providing deluxe accommodations for the dog and bird.

Deb Grant's Online Information:
**Email**: revdeb@jazzwater.com
**Website:** www.jazzwater.com
**Etsy Shop:** www.etsy.com/shop/Jazzwater
**Facebook:**
www.facebook.com/ElogosWordFoodbyDeb/
All of Grant's books are available on Amazon.